PAN
AND GRIDDLE
CAKES

by SAMUEL R. OGDEN

Illustrated by Nancy Miller

A Harvest Home Cookbook

THE STEPHEN GREENE PRESS
BRATTLEBORO, VERMONT

ACKNOWLEDGMENT: The recipes for *Landgrove Potato Pancakes* and *Immortal Corn Pancakes* are reprinted with permission from "Pancakes Worth Waiting For" from the *Berkshire Eagle—Upland Winter,* January-March, 1971 issue.

Copyright © 1973 by Samuel R. Ogden

Library of Congress Catalog Card Number: 73-82749
International Standard Book Number: 0-8289-0190-2

73 74 75 76 77 78 79 9 8 7 6 5 4 3 2 1

A Pancake Pilgrimage

My interest in pancakes stems from the lack of success I had in finding a restaurant that served good potato pancakes; or, in fact, any potato pancakes; nor could I find a recipe for the potato pancake of my dreams. This led to a culinary search of my own. After many tries, I finally devised a formula which produced the desired result (this, along with a recipe for corn pancakes, was published in *Upland Winter,* a local New England newspaper supplement, under the title "Pancakes Worth Waiting for").

At the start of my quest for the perfect pancake, I noted that seemingly no batter could be made without flour. This bothered me a bit: the tendency of flour to gather in lumps put me off, and the fact that the wallpaper paste of yesteryear was nothing more or less than flour and water put me off even more. Although this was a bit far-fetched, I could not but think there must be a better way.

Among other things I wondered if pulverized dried bread could not be substituted for flour to good advantage, and after some trial and error, I found that such was the case. So, in great measure, the batters formulated herein are based on the use of pulverized dried bread. In a way, this is the basic reason for this book, and the difference between it and others.

During my many hours of experimentation I discovered that, because of the constant requirement for a certain texture within the cakes themselves, there were times when flour could not be omitted. In some cases, the cakes, after being properly browned on one side, could not be turned without falling apart—a situation which could get even the best pancaker into a mess of trouble. In particular, when fruits were added to the basic formula, no amount of dickering with the consistency of the batter or the way the cakes were cooked could cure the trouble. In these instances my bread ingredient had to be either mixed with flour or eliminated entirely. And so I found that my use of pulverized bread was not a magic key to unlock all doors to perfect pancakes. Nevertheless, when properly used, it is my contention that dried bread results in improved cakes.

Types of Cakes

Although there are at least three general types of pan and griddle cakes, by far the largest number fall into the egg-flour-milk-butter-sugar-baking powder-batter category. In fact, the initial recipe in this collection is of this garden variety of flour-based pancake. This basic batter can then be modified by the addition of all sorts of fruits, vegetables, fish or meats, with each variation requiring certain alterations in the basic formula. Thus fortified the "lowly" pancake becomes something more resembling a griddle-fritter and makes an excellent light main-dish.

Beyond this, there is the lighter, generally baking powderless-batter which produces delectable thin cakes which might better be called confections. These are the dessert cakes, to be used to top off the meal, perhaps along with a glass of sweet white wine. Although these dessert cakes are indeed delicious, I will not give too much space to their refinement here. They are not my specialty. Perhaps you can take the basic recipes I have included and go from there.

I choose to put the balance of pan and griddle cakes in the sourdough category, wherein the batter is raised either by using yeast or a "starter" consisting of a specially-prepared fermented dough which is kept in a crock from one use to the next. These "sourdough" pancakes can also be varied as one wishes, but the sourdough is a stouter and heavier dish than the plain-batter variety, and is far removed from the confection cake. The supreme dish of my childhood consisted of several raised buckwheat pancakes liberally spread with country butter and "soft-sugar" (a concoction made on the farm consisting of maple syrup boiled just short of becoming hard sugar and which spreads like jam).

But times have changed: raised pancakes have become outmoded, succumbing, like many other delicious home-made dishes, to the ready-mixed trend of our times. Packaged pancake mixes are fine, for a good dish of pancakes doused with butter and swimming in pure Vermont maple syrup, gives a gustatory start to the day which can be matched in no other way, but nothing compares with the made-from-scratch variety—whether it be one of the ones from my little book or your own favorite. However, do try at least one of the sourdough varieties offered—for old times' sake, if nothing else.

Griddle & Cookery Hints

I recommend a soapstone griddle as it holds an even heat and stays hot longer. But good pancakes can be made on almost any griddle. Proper heating and greasing—often mysterious in pancake lore—*are* important but not so mysterious as legend has it. The test repeatedly given for proof of proper griddle heat is to drop a smidgin of cold water on the surface; the idea being that if the drops skitter around hopping up and down, the temperature is just right. (If too hot, the water disappears in a puff of steam; if not hot enough, it just sits there and simmers.) I must report—and I've flipped a lot of flapjacks—that I've never yet seen the hopping drops. That aside, it is not difficult to judge when the griddle is at proper heat. A bit of experience with your stove—whether gas, oil or electric—and your griddle will soon put you straight. If in doubt, a trial run with a small dollop of batter is a good means to check both the heat of the griddle and the consistency and seasoning of the batter.

The other side of the proper-griddle coin is proper greasing. Authorities will tell you that if you utter the right incantations it will not be necessary to use any grease on a soapstone griddle. All very well but I have found without exception that, without modest greasing, my pancakes stick. And besides, meeting the controversy head on, "what's wrong with greasing the griddle?" Perhaps rancid grease would harm the flavor of the cakes but what possible harm could result from the use of a bit of fresh butter?

As to the argument about cleaning the griddle, the honors seem evenly divided. To scrub the dry griddle off with salt (and I guess one should do it after each batch of cakes) is just as arduous as scouring the griddle when it is cool, or so it seems to me. But if you choose to divine by the way of jumping drops of water, or get some deep sense of satisfaction from cooking on the simon-pure stone, that's fine with me.

When trying my pulverized-bread-based recipes, be sure to use a firm-textured bread, cut in slices. Heat the slices in a moderate oven until they are hard and dry enough to crumble. Then roll with a rolling pin on a wooden board until the crumbs (hereafter called *pulv*) are fine. 4 to 5 slices of bread is generally adequate for the recipes in *Pan and Griddle Cakes* (4 slices makes about ¾ cup) but you can make the *pulv* in quantity and store it as it keeps a long while.

Whether *pulv*-based or flour-based, a well mixed batter is important. To meet this end a blender is a blessing for many pan and griddle cake recipes and I recommend the use of one for many of mine. One with adequate power is a must and one with removable blending blades is a great convenience for easy cleaning.

Proper timing when cooking pancakes is also important. Once the batter is spooned onto a properly heated griddle, little bubbles will soon form. When the bubbles that form around the perimeter burst, it is time to turn the cakes. Cooking on the reverse side will not take as long, so watch it.

The recipes offered in this little book have for the most part been tried by me—some of them several times. The rare exception is noted. Nearly all of them should serve 3 to 4 people, depending of course on how hearty the appetites.

Samuel R. Ogden
Landgrove, 1973

Plain Batter Cakes

1 cup flour
1 tablespoon baking powder
½ teaspoon salt
1 tablespoon sugar
3 tablespoons butter, melted
1 cup milk
2 eggs

Put the flour, baking powder, salt and sugar in a good-sized, preferably wooden, mixing bowl; stir together with a wooden spoon. Now stir in the melted butter, milk and eggs and mix the wet and dry ingredients together vigorously; however, if any lumps remain, they will not matter. Spoon the batter onto a lightly greased, hot griddle and cook, turning once when the little topside bubbles burst. *Makes 10 to 12 medium-sized griddle cakes.*

Served hot with syrup and a rasher of bacon or slice of ham, this batter makes tasty, stand-by breakfast fare.

Country Pancakes

½ teaspoon baking soda
½ teaspoon baking powder
½ teaspoon salt
1 tablespoon sugar
2 eggs
1 cup buttermilk
2 tablespoons butter, melted
1 cup flour

Mix together the baking soda, baking powder, salt and sugar in a wooden (if available) mixing bowl; add the eggs, buttermilk and butter, stirring all together thoroughly. Then beat in the flour until reasonably smooth; transfer to a blender and whirl until the batter is well blended. Cook on a hot, greased griddle, turning once. *Makes 10 to 12 medium-sized pancakes.*

This rule is a country cousin to the *Plain Batter Cakes.*

Corn Meal Pancakes

1 cup yellow corn meal
1 cup flour
1 tablespoon baking powder
1 tablespoon sugar
1 teaspoon salt
2 eggs
2 cups milk
4 tablespoons butter, melted

Mix the corn meal and flour together thoroughly; cut in the baking powder, sugar and salt. In a separate bowl, beat the eggs and stir in the milk and melted butter; stir this mixture into the dry ingredients and whirl in a blender until a smooth batter results. Cook on a hot griddle, turning once. *Makes 18 to 20 pancakes.*

Rice Pancakes

1 cup cooked rice
1 cup milk
½ teaspoon salt
5 tablespoons flour
2 teaspoons baking powder
2 tablespoons butter, melted
2 egg yolks, beaten

Keeping the eggs aside, combine the remaining ingredients in a mixing bowl; then fold in the beaten egg yolks. Cook on a hot griddle, turning once. *Makes 10 to 12 pancakes.*

This rule, one of the few I haven't tried myself, was given me by Tish Ferguson—that's endorsement enough.

† **Snow Pancakes:** *In her* Old Cook's Almanac *Bea Vaughan tells us how to make this up-country delicacy. Make a stiffer than usual pancake batter. Heat and grease the griddle. Then scoop up a cupful of immaculate snow for each cup of milk in the batter. Fold the snow into the batter quickly and cook as usual.*

Apple Griddle Cakes

1½ cups flour
1¼ teaspoons baking powder
¾ teaspoon salt
½ teaspoon cinnamon
¼ cup sugar
1 egg, beaten
1 cup milk
¼ cup butter, melted
1 cup apples, finely chopped

Sift and mix the dry ingredients. Stir together the egg, milk, butter and apples; add the dry ingredients and mix well until a smoothly-textured batter results. Fry on a hot greased griddle as before. *Makes 15 to 18 griddle cakes.*

This rule is from the kitchen of Demetria Taylor and passed along to me by Bobby Comfort. I have not prepared these *Apple Griddle Cakes* myself but understand they are delicious.

Kentucky Flannel Cakes

1¼ cups coffee cream
2 eggs, beaten
¼ teaspoon salt
2 tablespoons sugar
1 cup flour

Mix together all ingredients thoroughly until the batter is smooth. Fry on a hot, well-greased griddle, turning once as indicated. *Makes 12 to 15 medium-sized cakes.*

Sesame Pancakes

2 tablespoons olive oil
1 tablespoon chopped shallots (or onions)
½ cup *pulv* (pulverized dried bread)
1 tablespoon flour
½ cup buckwheat flour
1 cup milk
½ cup sour cream
1 egg
½ teaspoon salt
½ teaspoon baking soda
freshly-ground black pepper to taste
½ cup raw sesame seeds

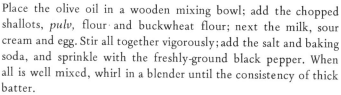

Place the olive oil in a wooden mixing bowl; add the chopped shallots, *pulv*, flour and buckwheat flour; next the milk, sour cream and egg. Stir all together vigorously; add the salt and baking soda, and sprinkle with the freshly-ground black pepper. When all is well mixed, whirl in a blender until the consistency of thick batter.

Preheat the griddle; grease with butter, olive oil or bacon fat and sprinkle with the sesame seeds. Spoon the batter onto the griddle and cook as before. *Makes 18 to 20 pancakes.*

Applesauce Pancakes

1 tablespoon olive oil
1½ cups *pulv* (pulverized dried bread)
1 cup sweet applesauce
2 eggs
2 tablespoons sour cream
½ cup coffee cream
½ teaspoon salt
freshly-ground black pepper to taste

Place all the ingredients in a wooden (if available) mixing bowl; stir until thoroughly blended and cook on a hot greased griddle as before. *Makes 18 to 20 pancakes.*

Bacon Pancakes

2 tablespoons olive oil
½ cup *pulv* (pulverized dried bread)
¾ cup lightly fried bacon, finely chopped
1 teaspoon salt
½ teaspoon freshly-ground black pepper
pinch of oregano
1 small clove garlic
2 cups cooked hominy grits
1 egg
1 cup milk

Place the olive oil in a preferably wooden mixing bowl; add the *pulv* and chopped bacon, together with the dry seasonings and the garlic; chop until fine. Now mix in the grits, egg and milk and stir all together until well mixed. Whirl the batter in a blender until smooth and fry on a well-greased hot griddle. *Makes 18 to 20 pancakes.*

Kipper Pancakes

2 (3¼-oz.) cans kippered fish fillets
2 raw potatoes, chopped
1 medium onion, chopped
1 cup *pulv* (pulverized dried bread)
2 eggs
1 cup milk

Oil a wooden chopping bowl; in this, chop the kippered fish, potatoes and onion fine; add the *pulv*, eggs and milk. Stir all together thoroughly, then whirl in a blender until the batter is smooth and fairly stiff. Cook on a hot greased griddle. *Makes 14 to 16 pancakes.*

This variation makes a tasty Sunday morning treat.

† **Pineapple Pancakes:** *Add ¼ cup well-drained canned crushed pineapple to the* Plain Batter Cakes.

My Blueberry Pancakes

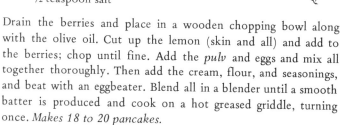

1 (15-oz.) can wild blueberries
2 tablespoons olive oil
¼ lemon
¾ cup *pulv* (pulverized dried bread)
2 eggs
1 cup coffee cream
1 cup flour
½ teaspoon white pepper
½ teaspoon salt

Drain the berries and place in a wooden chopping bowl along with the olive oil. Cut up the lemon (skin and all) and add to the berries; chop until fine. Add the *pulv* and eggs and mix all together thoroughly. Then add the cream, flour, and seasonings, and beat with an eggbeater. Blend all in a blender until a smooth batter is produced and cook on a hot greased griddle, turning once. *Makes 18 to 20 pancakes.*

When developing this rule, I had a little trouble with the texture of the cakes: made without flour, they tended to fall apart when turning them. On your first run, why not make a trial cake; if it tends to crumble, add a little more flour.

Bobby Comfort's Blueberry Pancakes

1 teaspoon baking soda
2 cups thick sour milk
2 eggs, well beaten
1½ cups fresh blueberries
2½ cups flour
½ teaspoon salt
2 tablespoons butter, melted

Dissolve the soda in a small amount of warm water and add to the milk. Beat and add the eggs. Crush the blueberries with a wooden spoon and add to the milk-egg mixture; stir in the flour, salt and melted butter and mix well. Spoon the batter on to a hot greased griddle and cook as before. *Makes 22 to 24 pancakes.*

Old Fashioned Buckwheat Cakes

1 packet dried yeast
2 cups lukewarm water
2 cups buckwheat flour
½ cup white flour
1 teaspoon salt
1 cup milk
1 teaspoon baking soda

Dissolve the yeast in part of the water. Mix the flours, salt, and milk with the balance of the water. Then add in the dissolved yeast and beat until smooth; let rise overnight or for 6 to 7 hours. Just before cooking, add the soda, stirring well. Grease the griddle with bacon grease or butter, and cook as before. *Makes 18 to 20 buckwheat cakes.*

Raised Buckwheat Pancakes

1 packet dried yeast
3 tablespoons molasses
2¼ cups lukewarm water
1 cup milk
1½ teaspoons salt
2 cups buckwheat flour
1 cup white flour, sifted

In a fairly large bowl, dissolve the yeast and molasses in the lukewarm water. Scald the milk, add the salt and cool to lukewarm; add to the dissolved yeast. Then add the buckwheat and white flours gradually, beating until smooth. Cover all and let rise in a warm place, free from draft, until light—about 1 hour. Stir the batter well and fry as for regular pancakes. *Makes 18 to 20 buckwheat cakes.*

A good raised buckwheat batter can be made overnight. Prepare as above but use only ¼ packet of yeast and add an extra ½ teaspoon of salt. When the batter is mixed, let it stand covered overnight in a cool place.

AUTHOR'S ASIDE: Having misplaced my mother's old-time rule for sourdough pancakes, I devised this recipe just for this book. It's a lot of work but offers a welcome taste of days gone by.

Sourdough Buckwheat Cakes

Starter:
3 cups potato water (water in which
 potatoes have been boiled)
1 cup white flour
1 packet dry yeast

Dough:
3 cups *starter*
1 cup buckwheat flour
1 cup white flour
1 cup warm water
2 tablespoons olive oil
1 egg
1 cup milk (or ¼ cup evaporated milk plus
 ¾ cup water)
1 teaspoon salt
1 teaspoon baking soda
2 tablespoons sugar

To prepare the sourdough *starter,* first prepare the potato water, adding 1 teaspoon of butter to the cooking water and preferably using potatoes with their jackets on. Then mix the potato water, flour and yeast together well and let stand in a warm place until fermented (about 2 days); cover and keep cool until just before using.

To make the dough, place the *starter* in a large bowl; add the flours and warm water and mix thoroughly. Cover and let stand in a warm place overnight (10 to 12 hours). Then add the olive oil, egg and milk; mix well again until the dough is smooth. Combine separately the salt, baking soda and sugar, and scatter evenly over the batter, stirring in gently. When the bubbling is over (stir occasionally) let the dough sit for 5 minutes or so before spooning onto a preheated and buttered griddle. (Spread some butter on the griddle until it starts to smoke, then turn down the heat a bit.) If the batter is too thin, thicken with flour; if too thick, thin with milk. *Serves from 4 to 5 good appetites.*

Because of the sour taste a sweet syrup is a must with sourdough buckwheat cakes.

Important note: Do not use all of the batter; set aside 1 full cup to use as future sourdough *starter.* Put the batter in a jar, add 2 cups of potato water and keep warm until fermented; cover and keep cool until ready to use again.

Ellen Orton's Quick Buckwheat Cakes

1 cup buckwheat flour
½ teaspoon baking soda
¾ teaspoon salt
½ cup sour cream
1 cup milk, approximate

Mix the buckwheat flour, baking soda and salt, then add the sour cream and enough milk to make a thin batter. When cooking, remember the rule for buckwheat cakes—a hot, well-greased griddle. *Makes 10 to 12 cakes.*

Plain Buckwheat Cakes

1 cup buckwheat flour
½ cup brown sugar
1 teaspoon soda
½ teaspoon baking powder
½ cup thick sour cream
2 eggs
½ cup coffee cream
½ teaspoon salt
½ teaspoon freshly-ground pepper

Stir all the ingredients together vigorously in a mixing bowl with a wooden spoon until well combined; then whirl in a blender. The blender step can be eliminated, but I prefer it to be sure the eggs and sour cream are thoroughly integrated into the batter. Cook on a hot well-greased griddle, thinning the batter with a bit of milk if necessary. *Makes 10 to 12 cakes.*

very tasty - reminds me of mayo cake but not
chocolate — very fluffy 15 - and difficult to get
spatula under for turning — absorb syrups
instantly - need melted butter as they tear
easily!

Brunch Pancakes

1 cup shredded Swiss cheese
2 tablespoons flour
1 tablespoon mustard
2 eggs, beaten
½ cup sour cream

Mix the cheese, flour and mustard. Then mix the eggs and sour cream together. Combine the two mixes, and when thoroughly mixed, fry in small cakes on a hot greased griddle. *Makes 10 to 12 pancakes.*

Nancy Rice, the provider of this recipe, recommends that these pancakes be served with sliced chicken breast in Mornay sauce.

Vermont Cheese Pancakes

2 tablespoons olive oil
1 cup shredded Vermont cheddar cheese
1 cup *pulv* (pulverized dried bread)
1 cup chopped spanish onions
2 eggs
1 tablespoon sugar
½ teaspoon salt
½ teaspoon freshly-ground pepper
4 teaspoons flour
½ teaspoon baking powder
1 cup beer

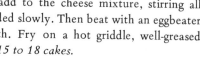

Place the olive oil in a wooden chopping bowl and chop in the shredded cheese, the *pulv*, the onions and the eggs. Mix together the dry ingredients and add to the cheese mixture, stirring all together as the beer is added slowly. Then beat with an eggbeater until the batter is smooth. Fry on a hot griddle, well-greased with bacon grease. *Makes 15 to 18 cakes.*

Sour Cream Pancakes

1 tablespoon olive oil
1 tablespoon chopped parsley
1 cup *pulv* (pulverized dried bread)
2 eggs
1½ cups sour cream
½ cup coffee cream
½ teaspoon freshly-ground black pepper
½ teaspoon salt

First oil a wooden bowl; in this, chop the parsley, very fine. Add the *pulv* and eggs, chopping them in as well. Then mix in the sour cream and the cream; add the seasonings and stir thoroughly. Cook as before. *Makes 15 to 18 pancakes.*

Cottage Cheese Pancakes

1 tablespoon olive oil
3 eggs
1 cup cottage cheese
1 cup sour cream
¼ teaspoon salt
1 scant teaspoon pepper, freshly ground
¾ cup *pulv* (pulverized bread)
1 tablespoon sugar

Oil a wooden bowl; beat the eggs therein and add the cheese and cream. Add the seasonings, *pulv* and sugar and stir until the batter is thoroughly mixed. Cook on a hot, greased griddle as before. *Makes 14 to 16 pancakes.*

† *You might try dipping pancake batter with a ¼-cup measure—or using a tablespoon for dollar-size cakes.*

† *One way to keep pancakes hot is to place them, covered but with lid ajar, in a heavy pan over a very low heat. Or they can be placed on a rack in a shallow pan for a short time in a very slow (250) oven.*

Landgrove Potato Pancakes

5 cups raw potatoes, peeled and
  cut in small pieces
2 tablespoons olive oil
1 clove garlic (optional)
1 medium onion
2 tablespoons minced parsley
¾ cup *pulv* (pulverized bread)
2 eggs
1 teaspoon salt
1 teaspoon black pepper, freshly ground
¼ cup coffee cream

Put the peeled potato pieces in cold water. Then oil a wooden
bowl with the olive oil. Peel the garlic and chop very fine in the
bowl along with the onion and parsley; chop in the *pulv* and eggs
and mix. Put the bits of potato through a meat grinder (medium
blade), saving all the juice. (The potatoes can be halved and grated
but I prefer the grinder.) Add the ground potatoes and juice to
the *pulv*-onion mixture along with the seasonings and stir thoroughly. When well mixed, add the cream and place in a blender; whirl
until the batter is stiff and smooth. Butter a griddle and try a
small dollop as a pilot cake. *Makes 20 to 22 small pancakes.*

    I cook six or eight at a time, placing them on a hot platter
until the balance are done and then serve all at once—with cold
corned brisket or pastrami and applesauce as a side dish.

Luchow's Potato Pancakes

2 pounds (6) medium-sized potatoes
½ medium-sized onion, grated
2 tablespoons flour
2 eggs, beaten
1½ teaspoons salt
½ teaspoon pepper
¼ teaspoon ground nutmeg
2 tablespoons minced parsley

3 to 4 tablespoons butter
4 strips bacon, cooked crisp

Wash and peel the potatoes; cover with cold water and drain; grate at once and drain off any accumulated water. Place in a bowl; add the onion and mix. Add the flour, eggs, salt, pepper, nutmeg and parsley and mix thoroughly. Heat the butter on a griddle or in a large frying pan. Ladle out large spoonfuls of the potato mixture onto the hot pan or griddle; bake three or four pancakes at one time until brown and crisp on each side, turning with a pancake turner. Place on a hot dish and garnish with crisp bacon. *Serves 6.*

This fine recipe is courtesy of Mrs. Joseph Levine who recommends serving stewed apples with these pancakes.

Potato Mushroom Pancakes

½ pound mushrooms
4 medium potatoes
1 medium onion
1 egg
1 teaspoon salt
1/8 teaspoon white pepper
1 teaspoon corn starch
2 tablespoons flour
1 teaspoon baking powder

Peel the potatoes, slice or dice and purée in a blender; drain in a paper towel in a sieve. Grate the onion in a large bowl; add the egg and other ingredients, except for the mushrooms, along with the drained potatoes. When the batter is stirred smooth, slice the mushrooms very fine and fold into the batter. Cook in a skillet in ¼ inch of hot oil, and drain briefly on a paper towel when cooked. *Makes 14 to 16 pancakes.*

This recipe has been all-around Robin Hood's barn—from Rosette Reitz to Bobby Comfort to me. I'm told these *Potato Mushroom Pancakes* are best served with sour cream or yogurt.

Chicken Liver-stuffed Pancake Rolls

½ pound chicken livers
1½ cups water
1 cube chicken bouillon
1 cup milk
4 tablespoons melted butter or
  margarine
5 tablespoons flour
½ teaspoon salt
small pinch of salt

Cook the livers in the water, to which the bouillon cube has been added; when tender (about 15 minutes), drain, reserving the broth. Cut up the livers coarsely. Combine the milk with 1 cup of the broth. Blend the melted butter and flour; add the broth-milk mixture and stir over a low heat until thick and smooth; add the salt and pepper. To the cut-up livers, add enough of the sauce, about ¾ cup, to make rather moist. Keep hot, keeping remainder of the sauce hot as well.

Using the *Thin Pancakes* (below), place a spoonful of the liver mixture in the center of each cooked cake, roll and keep hot. *Makes enough mixture to fill about 4 to 6 cakes.*

Serve with the reserved sauce spooned over each portion.

Thin Pancakes

¾ cup sifted flour
½ teaspoon salt
1 teaspoon baking powder
2 eggs, beaten
2/3 cup milk
1/3 cup water

Sift the dry ingredients into a bowl; add the beaten eggs, milk and water all at once. Mix all together with a few rapid strokes but don't beat. Brush a 5-inch frying pan with a little oil and place over a medium heat. When hot, add just enough of the batter to cover the bottom of the pan with a thin coating, tipping the pan from side to side to spread the batter evenly; cook over a moderate heat, turning each pancake when browned on the under side. Be sure to grease the pan between each cake. *Makes 8 to 10 pancakes.* This rule is based on one from the incomparable Bea Vaughan and found in her *Ladies Aid Cookbook.*

Salt Cod Pancakes

1½ cups dried salted codfish, freshened
1 tablespoon olive oil
1½ cups *pulv* (pulverized bread)
2 eggs
1 teaspoon pepper, freshly ground
pinch of dried tarragon
2 cups milk

It does not take as much time and trouble to freshen salt codfish as you may believe. First, wash the fish in cold water, getting rid of all the salt and any extraneous bits. Then shred or cut it into small pieces and proceed. Soak the fish in hot water for 20 minutes; change the water and soak again for another 20 minutes. Cover the soaked fish with hot water, bring to a boil and cook until tender; when done, allow to drain and dry on paper toweling. Place the oil in a wooden chopping bowl; add the fish, chopping it fine. Then add the *pulv,* break in the eggs and seasoning and thoroughly stir in the milk. Place the batter in a blender and whirl until smooth. Cook on a hot, greased griddle as before. *Makes 18 to 20 pancakes.*
These are very fine, indeed.

† *Some experts say that if the pancake recipe contains 2 or more tablespoons of shortening for each cup liquid, you won't need to grease the griddle.*

† *If one is calorie conscious—and who isn't these days—there are 60 calories in one 4-inch plain-batter griddle cake, but only about 45 calories in one 4-inch buckwheat griddle cake. It is the syrups and sauces that add the calories.*

Clam Pancakes

1 (8-oz.) can minced clams
1 cup *pulv* (pulverized bread)
1 medium onion, chopped
1 pinch rosemary
½ teaspoon black pepper, freshly ground
½ teaspoon salt
½ cup coffee cream

Place all the ingredients in a mixing bowl and stir thoroughly; put in a blender and whirl until the batter is smooth. Cook on a hot, greased griddle as before. *Makes 10 to 12 pancakes.*

† Half-and-half is half cream and half milk. It is used in coffee, or for table use. It can be substituted for light cream in recipes.

Corned Beef Pancakes

¾ cup sliced corn beef, shredded fine
1 cup boiled potatoes
½ cup chopped raw onions
2 tablespoons olive oil
2 eggs
1 cup *pulv* (pulverized dried bread)
1 teaspoon baking powder dissolved in
    4 tablespoons water
1½ cups coffee cream
salt and pepper to taste

Chop the corned beef, potatoes and onions together with the olive oil in a wooden bowl. Combine the eggs with the *pulv* and baking-powder solution; add to the meat mixture and mix all together with the coffee cream. Place the batter in a blender and whirl until smooth. Season the batter while still in the blender with the salt and freshly-ground pepper. Cook on a hot greased griddle as before. *Makes 14 to 16 cakes.*

Chipped Beef Pancakes

¾ cup chipped beef, cut up fine
1 tablespoon olive oil
1 medium-sized clove garlic, finely chopped
1 cup dried celery leaves (or 1 teaspoon
   celery salt)
2 teaspoons finely-chopped parsley
½ teaspoon baking powder
2 tablespoons flour
1 cup *pulv* (pulverized dried bread)
1 egg
1 cup coffee cream

Place the oil in the bottom of a wooden chopping bowl and chop the chipped beef into it along with the garlic. Then add the celery leaves or celery salt, followed by the parsley, baking powder, flour and *pulv*. Mix all together and add the egg and cream. Stir well and then whirl in a blender until the batter is smooth. Cook on a hot, greased griddle. *Makes 12 to 14 pancakes.*

Winter Squash Pancakes

1 cup squash meat
½ cup maple syrup
1 cup *pulv* (pulverized dried bread)
½ cup flour
3 teaspoons corn starch
¼ cup dark rum

Boil gold nugget or butternut squash and scrape the soft meat into a cup; mix with the maple syrup, *pulv*, flour and corn starch. Add the rum and stir until well mixed, then whirl in a blender until smooth. Cook on a well-greased hot griddle. *Makes 12 to 15 pancakes.*

Immortal Corn Pancakes

2 tablespoons olive oil
3 cups corn kernels, cut from
    freshly-cooked cobs
3 tablespoons chopped onion
1 teaspoon salt
1 teaspoon black pepper, freshly ground
1 cup *pulv* (pulverized bread)
2 eggs
1 cup coffee cream

Put the olive oil in a wooden bowl and add the corn. Then add the onion, seasonings and *pulv* and chop until fine; add the eggs and cream and stir vigorously. When well mixed, whirl in a blender until a thick, smooth batter is obtained. Cook on a hot, greased griddle as before. *Makes 18 to 20 pancakes.*

If freshly-cooked corn-on-the-cob is not available, canned or frozen corn will do; use the niblet variety.

Tomato Pancakes

1 tablespoon olive oil
1 small onion
2 cups canned stewed tomatoes
1 cup coffee cream
1 teaspoon black pepper, freshly ground
1 teaspoon salt
1 tablespoon baking soda
1 tablespoon sugar
1½ cups flour

Place the oil in a wooden chopping bowl; add the onion and chop very fine. Add in the tomatoes and cream and mix all together thoroughly. In a separate bowl combine the dry ingredients, adding in the flour last; add the dry ingredients to the tomato-onion mixture and mix thoroughly, either by hand or in a blender. Then cook on a hot, greased griddle as before. *Makes 14 to 16 pancakes.*

Parsnip Pancakes

3 cups parsnips, peeled and cut in pieces
1 cup Bermuda onion, cut in pieces
1 cup *pulv* (pulverized dried bread)
2 tablespoons butter, melted
1 teaspoon freshly-ground pepper
½ teaspoon salt

Boil the parsnip and onion in a saucepan for 1 hour; drain and mash together with a potato masher. When the consistency of a purée, cool and add the *pulv,* butter and seasonings. Place the batter in a blender and whirl until smooth. Cook on a hot, greased griddle as before. *Makes 16 to 18 pancakes.*

Green Pepper and Onion Pancakes

1 tablespoon olive oil
3½ cups chopped onions
1 medium green pepper, chopped
½ teaspoon salt
freshly-ground black pepper to taste
oregano to taste
½ tablespoon butter
¾ cup *pulv* (pulverized bread)
½ tablespoon baking powder
1 cup flour
½ tablespoon bacon grease
1 egg

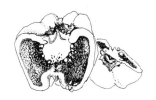

Place the olive oil in a wooden bowl and chop in the onion and pepper until fine. Transfer this mixture to an iron skillet, just covering with water. Add the salt, pepper, oregano and butter and bring to a boil; simmer until soft and drain. Combine the *pulv*, baking powder, flour and bacon grease; add in the vegetable mixture and chop all together until very fine. Then mix in the egg, adding some of the onion-pepper water if needed to make a smooth batter. *Makes 18 to 20 pancakes.*

Cabbage and Rum Pancakes

1 tablespoon olive oil
1 clove garlic
2 cups sliced raw cabbage
¼ lemon, including the rind
2 eggs
1 cup *pulv* (pulverized bread)
½ cup sour cream
1 tablespoon sugar
½ teaspoon black pepper, freshly ground
½ teaspoon salt
½ cup coffee cream
1½ tablespoons dark rum

Chop the garlic, cabbage and lemon all very fine in a wooden chopping bowl together with the olive oil; mix in the eggs, *pulv* and sour cream until thoroughly blended. Add the sugar and seasonings, and transfer all to a blender; top with the rum and coffee cream and blend until the batter is smooth. Proceed to fry on a hot, greased griddle as before. *Makes 16 to 18 cakes.*

Peanut Butter Pancakes

1 tablespoon olive oil
1 cup peanut butter
1 egg
1 cup coffee cream
1 cup *pulv* (pulverized bread)
1 tablespoon chopped parsley

Place the olive oil in a wooden bowl together with the peanut butter and egg. Mix all together with a wooden spoon; when thoroughly mixed, add in the cream and *pulv*, together with the chopped parsley. Stir into a batter of proper consistency, adding a bit more cream if necessary. *Makes 10 to 12 pancakes.*

The Pancake

4 tablespoons butter
½ cup milk
2 eggs
½ cup flour

Set the oven at 425. Place the butter in a 12-inch iron skillet and heat very hot. Combine the eggs, milk and flour in a mixing bowl and beat slightly; lumps will not matter. Pour the batter into the skillet and place in the oven; bake 15 to 20 minutes and serve at once. For dessert, fill with a mixture of frozen strawberries (1 [7-oz.] package), thickened with 1 tablespoon of corn starch and a jar of currant jelly, or with ice cream topped with raspberry sauce. *Serves 2.*

For breakfast, this same pancake can be served with maple syrup or jam; for luncheon, filled with creamed crab, lobster, chicken or mushrooms.

This recipe was given me by Nancy Rice and Lil Swan.

Pancake Nonpareil

½ cup flour
½ cup milk
2 eggs, slightly beaten
pinch of nutmeg
4 tablespoons butter
2 tablespoons confectioner's sugar
juice of ½ lemon

Preheat the oven to 425. In a mixing bowl, combine the flour, milk, eggs and nutmeg; beat lightly, leaving the batter a little lumpy. Melt the butter in a 12-inch skillet with a heat-proof handle. When very hot, pour in the batter; bake in the oven 15 to 20 minutes, or until golden brown. Sprinkle with the sugar and return briefly to the oven. Sprinkle with lemon juice and serve with jelly, jam or marmalade. *Serves 2 or 3.*

Freddy Harris gave me this nice rule.

Raspberry Pancakes

1½ cups unsweetened thick raspberry purée
1 cup ricotta or cottage cheese
2 tablespoons cream cheese, softened
3 eggs
¼ cup sugar
¼ teaspoon salt
¼ cup milk
2/3 cup all-purpose flour, sifted
2 tablespoons butter, melted

Rub the raspberry purée and cheeses through a fine sieve. Beat the eggs, sugar and salt until thick, then add and thoroughly beat in the raspberry-cheese mixture. Beat in the milk until smooth, then gradually add the flour, beating until smooth after each addition. Stir in the melted butter, mixing well, and cook on a hot, greased griddle until lightly browned on each side. *Makes 12 to 14 pancakes.*

I do not know where this recipe came from, and have not tried it, but it sounds so delicious I thought I would offer it here.

French Pancakes

3 eggs, separated
1 teaspoon sugar
½ teaspoon salt
1 cup milk
½ cup flour, sifted
1 tablespoon butter, melted

Beat the egg yolks; add the sugar, salt and ½ of the milk. Stir in the sifted flour, the balance of the milk and the melted butter. Beat the egg whites stiff and fold in gently. Fry on a lightly greased, hot griddle, making a large pancake. Turn; when brown, remove to a warmed platter. Spread with currant jelly, roll up and sprinkle with powdered sugar. *Serves 2 or 3.*

This tempting rule is courtesy of Nancy Rice.

Jamaica Banana Pancakes

1 egg
1 teaspoon sugar
3 teaspoons flour
½ teaspoon baking powder
3 ripe bananas, mashed

Beat the egg and sugar together, add the flour, baking powder and banana and mix lightly with a fork. These dessert cakes cook quickly. Sprinkle with powdered sugar. *Serves 3 or 4.*
This recipe was given me by Bobby Comfort—a trusted fellow-chef.

Blinis

Pancake mix:	*Filling:*
2 eggs	1 pound cottage cheese
1/3 cup flour	8 ounces cream cheese
¼ cup water	1 egg
¼ cup milk	1 tablespoon *pulv* (pulverized bread)

Combine the pancake mix ingredients in a blender. Heat a heavy 10- or 12-inch frying pan. Run a frozen stick of butter quickly over the pan; tip the pan up off the stove and pour in about ½ cup of the pancake mix, pouring back that which does not adhere to the pan. Fry until lightly browned on both sides and invert quickly onto a well-buttered china dinner plate. Repeat this procedure for each cake and stack on the plate.

Combine the filling ingredients, mixing until smooth. Fill each pancake with this mixture and fold toward the center four times, envelope fashion. Sauté each lightly in butter and serve on a hot plate with sour cream and jelly. *Makes 12 blinis.*

This tempting recipe was given me by Hortense Mizner.

Author's note: Blinis can also be filled with caviar or sour cream Russian-style and served as an appetizer.

Old Fashioned Maple

Certainly still the first and foremost of all pan and griddle cake toppings is the veritable pure Vermont maple syrup—the merchandising of which is now regulated by law so that the buyer may be certain he gets what he pays for.

This old favorite comes in different grades: Fancy, A, and B, plus a darker commercial grade used for such things as chewing tobacco, maple candy and the various blends of table syrup. For everyday table use I recommend the lighter Fancy, in spite of its somewhat higher cost and the widespread notion that the darker the syrup the more it tastes like maple.

There is nothing wrong with the several types of packaged syrups—blended from a combination of various sweet syrups and flavored with synthetic maple flavoring—and they are easier on the budget—but they do not have the old-fashioned maple taste.

Caramel Syrup

½ cup sugar
corn syrup as needed

Place the sugar in a small iron frying pan; brown this slowly over a modest heat until it is caramelized, adding water as necessary to keep from sticking. The result should be a sweet thin brown liquid with a distinctly caramel taste. Add to this enough corn syrup to give the syrup a good rich consistency. *Makes ¾ to 1 cup.*

The corn syrup used should be as tasteless as possible and not too sweet.

Brown Sugar Syrup

1/3 cup butter
1 cup brown sugar
1 cup half and half coffee cream
optional: ¼ cup bourbon

Cream the butter in a medium-sized sauce pan; add the brown sugar and cream again thoroughly. Heat the coffee cream; add gradually to the butter-sugar mixture and cook until boiling. Remove from the heat and, if you wish, add the bourbon. Beat all together with an egg beater until smooth. *Makes 2 or more cups.* This syrup is more suitable for the light dessert cakes than for breakfast pancakes.

Blueberry Sauce

4 teaspoons cornstarch
½ cup sugar
1 cup water
1 teaspoon lemon juice
1 cup fresh blueberries
1 tablespoon butter
optional: ¼ teaspoon cinnamon

Blend the cornstarch and sugar in a medium-sized saucepan. Add the next 3 ingredients; stir and cook the mixture over a low heat until thick and transparent. Add the butter, and cinnamon if desired, and serve warm. *Makes 1 1/3 cups.*
The cinnamon adds a spicy touch—nice for a change.

† **For Molasses Fanciers:** *Try one of the lighter and less bitter grades of molasses for a change-of-pace pancake topping.*

† *Crepe Suzettes are thin sweet pancakes usually served rolled, with a sweet hot orange or tangerine sauce, and flavored with curacao or other liqueurs.*

Yogurt-Horseradish Sauce

½ cup plain yogurt
1 tablespoon sour cream
2 teaspoons horseradish

Mix the ingredients together thoroughly and serve over dessert pancakes. *Makes ¾ cup.*

Use the in-vinegar style horseradish, not the cream style, for this tasty sauce.

Lemon Sauce

1/3 cup sugar
1 tablespoon cornstarch
1 cup water
4 tablespoons butter
½ teaspoon grated lemon rind
1½ tablespoons lemon juice
pinch of salt

Stir the sugar, cornstarch and water over a moderate heat until thickened. Add the remaining ingredients, stir and serve warm over dessert pancakes. *Makes 1½ cups.*

† **For Honey Lovers:** *Strained honey makes a most acceptable pancake topping—but this is perhaps the most expensive alternative of all.*